CONTINUITY

CONTINUITY

BY CYNTHIA ARRIEU-KING

Octopus Books
Portland, Oregon
2021

OCTOPUS
BOOKS

Continuity
© 2021 Cynthia Arrieu-King

First edition, 2021
ISBN: 978-1-7334551-1-4
Printed & bound in the USA

Cover image "Forest Smoke" by Corinna Berndt
corinnaberndt.net

Cover and layout design by Ken Miranda
kenmiranda.com

Octopus Books
Portland, Oregon
octopusbooks.net

CONTENTS

There ain't no normal life, Wyatt. It's just life.

-Doc Holliday, Tombstone

The beginning of the war will be secret.

-Jenny Holzer

Things as they are as it is—

-Suzuki Roshi

TWO OLD SELVES

The elderly swept their arms up in unison.
Pushing up the heavens. Lion growing. Mist sinking into the horizon.

At night, the stars chucked plentiful
against blackness, full of discount lightning.

Hectic Manhattan's Chinatown, that
drawer of sidewalk and rings, no
room to pass either side.

Five billion people, those were the days.

To cover the world with more apples
to cover the ground around back porches
and also to show
what and who endures in
this nowhere pavilion of necessities
I awoke, shining—

outside the city, at night a lake's alarm
an apple that played a lunar light
I saw two selves
the one faithful to history
and one who prefers the actual
they walk away from the corner
each down separate roads

the best moment for calling the ancestors—

for asking for clarity on how to change suffering to nothing

or whether that is the goal

Ask yourself when making these nail and yarn dolls—

you, so disappointed by the strangleholds of evil men—

Do I wish the person this doll represents some harm or some good?

CONTINUITY

A making-of about a samurai movie.
A fake half-a-limb cleans an embrace, or it waits.

A sudden fear of price, the full black element of garment;
A script girl picking through the smoke and dummies,
    ticks off lists.
Her hand arranges a subtle match; making story versus
    all this freight.
A studio workshop builds and glues hair to fake drowned rats.

And a man enters frame, the samurai actor in a parka fingers
    a cigarette, half-pirouettes, falls to the ground.
And then again he enters frame and practices this turn
    around the lake.

And it wasn't that long before, watching him,

        I wanted some ledge of words to rest on.

My brother throws a dish on the floor and it bounces.

Throws it again, it bounces.

This thing we stood in the kitchen trying to prove breaks (ages ago)

  though the warranty says, "unbreakable."

How the plate bounced the first time, bounced the second time.

The plate of one side and another that will never

face two sides of an argument. I pace back

and my brother's foot comes down hard,

the dish crinkles to thin teeth.

And what had seemed such a daily moon shreds to needles.

And who will save this blood data, beat the maze?

The way my brother would show me, actor in rehearsal,
    where to spike a throat with a pen

for maximum harm, it wasn't about starting a trache. The other
    brother laughs at a video I realize is a man being tased.

The actor gets up and does it again;
All these doctors doctoring, walking around in my heart.

Says the script girl: So much on the battlefield that doesn't jump—
that pins its rigid shawls   time long and slightly open

The degree to which brothers are wrong, the degree to which
    they are right
The degree to which they are wrong, the degree to which
    I am right.

Being with my dad's body the last time, sobbing on his plaid robe,
thinking *better get it all out now, no more practicing;*
    smaller, yellow, the hands drawn around
something that's not practice—

Some time after, I recall the shattered jaw:
How someone had been in a wreck, how he'd threaded
wire into the jawbone, had made careful incisions,

and with the snapped bone threaded, had pulled it taut:
how he loved when the flesh slid from a mess back into a face.

The director surveys the damage, what the workmen heard

The real sound of a story being told

The real sound of acting

a false "ancient" in false battalions.

All the samurai horses and armor walking beside the Sentras.

The features of history broken into soft thoughts,

what dress-up drill, this practice shot.

The script-girl out near these foam horses, tightening their lids.

This continuity woman touches a ticket to a heap in mud,

    snaps a Polaroid, logs it all

that one who tries to piece it together, who beats dust from

a neon parka zipped up to a glued-on beard,

    who improves death itself,

who herself has seen the good and bad ways to change a face.

[So from screaming it turned into things like blaming it all]

So from screaming it turned into things like blaming it all: an axe through the garage panels, the antipathy of white. Chips scraped from the garage side, rained down, the lawn's green blades up, the clean white board splintered and falling. Where could rage go? The noise of the axe through the wood over and over, a prayer cried into a pillow to make it stop and no pattern resolved, no rescue to relieve the scene. So many times, ignoring for the sake of normal: the bent forks and bent barbells. And the scream held at a note stretches into something airy, fades to something sung. The sheen of stares, spangles: hurt drops its age. Stage light and the chorus going until the repetition, hundred- fold. This goes and goes for years. You tire of a song; for you, it can no longer be heard.

JIU JITSU DÉÇU

Being human means feelings, burying anger in an essay
The woman strangled with her own rope

Some possible futures of English
Will have
Will

a pause to empty the head of expectations

say a boy in a white outfit *go* tries to throw his friend
and the mat slides, part water and salt

backed out of the driveway, trying to gain purchase in snow
no go

or:

So, that was winter
and the blossoms cough out their lilacs

I spend time in conversations wondering if I'm listening enough

she realized all that training was not going to make a difference—
cried for an hour then one more

his hands past my ears
my wrists under his hands
I realized all the training amounts to me immobile—

This conjuring act
            woman at bus stop   glint of piercing neon
            murmurs a sexy "seems like it" to the phone

such plain day

and the hardening of hands

and the sudden inability to flip to the end of a song.
(Must I listen to the whole song?)

FIX

The restaurants crammed at every hour with well-groomed people eating
London broil. The sheen on their hair. Unbreakable glass. You can hear the
asteroid coming. The water lead-filled. The air too hot. And dear left eye,
please stop shakin', babe, it's ok. Even the hour when the birds start chirping
makes a hyphen between words. A corrective to things haphazard. In
listening and wakefulness, no sound from anything, no one in the street
loading the air with curses or cures, I go for the brightest thing I can stand,
click "complete order."

EVERYBODY BELIEVES
THEY ARE THE GOOD GUY

After all the humans are gone, grandparents in a kindergarten

and the teacher draw an accordion wall across

to keep the children in anti-gravity class together;

the grandparents each grade balloon worksheets. Sunlight floats in,

the android grandparents thoughtful about addition, mulling vacation

Come here I said to the little one too little to be in floating class

I want to tell you something and you repeat it back to me next time

She toddled over, put her arms up to hug me, we hugged.

Under her coat was no body, only space and a white planet.

Repeat after me: more human than a human, got it? I cuddled her.

A bus in a strange galaxy shows, in its windows, more familiar faces.

Okay, she said, *I'm more human than a human.*

MOON IN REARVIEW

I sat in a stadium in the future—

an airplane

steered into its dangers

fiery   chased by another thing: a moon

their collision on a loop, the two smashing each other

looked real   until the hologram shuddered

    into a girl's senior project

the fuselage and tail flattened, a projected

repetition of an accident   /catastrophe

Pedestrians walked past as if

on their way to lunch

I told the student at my sign-up table each question

    she was about to ask me,

until she put on her shades and looked away

*

everything had changed so much

there were a few things that hadn't

it was still the same moon as had been in the back window

late, still acting as if it hoped to follow, or to mind

we still sat on sofas, had gravity, tides

but I was crossing things off that list each day   elemental

and the old worries gave way to the four seconds of microwaves through the city

an inability to surprise us   anymore our reflex was to get our bearings

where's the sky   where's the floor   where's the potable water

*

When I was four, my mother and brother took me into a dark room

one had a flashlight and a moon grapefruit

the other a basketball earth to show me why the moon

got black   got little

hung like it watches   subtly moors   (but moved with us)

the idea too big   window into the elemental

how was I supposed to know

how good this pocked knob in the rearview,

someone to give nighttime regards to and there's a pause

this figurine of ruined world   of ruining it just by being here:

no legal mud, no soot

I look to the moon   that same moon

its pull on water   its pull on sanity

how much further away she rests

than most people assume

VEIL FROM ANAPOS

you throw this pretend net on your brother and struggle to keep him still

his face a grammatical diagram under veil   playing wild hermit

when you stamped on the blanket edges   a safety-zone wildflower field

a thing made for proving clouds—

cloud and its remainder—

this veil with apertures   five or a thousand of them—

fine lines compose this thing,   your hair kept back   wind

you kept a net   you kept   him covered   and down

throw this veil on ancestors and find the seams empty

their faces: what you have left in photos

the word pure obsolete   blood's a mixed drink and what loops back

cottons onto report & an umbilical anchor—

nearing your answers, you wrestle the covered hands and arms

your brother used

to keep you from falling

HOPE IS THE MOTHER
OF THE STUPID

Distant chatter, blue

and one cloud breaks

this clear water of injury

I'd never cried from pain before

another cell phone scenario

That's not what I said

That's not how it's spelled

By the end of a day—escarole, the never o'clock

the being hobbled by fiery pins; note to self

don't ever do paper-piecing again

it pinches, the agony of detergent.

My shoulder cartilage ragged,

I wonder if the binding hex worked—

or if the curse found a way

in my dreams to rest that

didn't hurt. Each morning,

as if at the start of a film,

I breathed in the pleasure

of waking soft, free, a blue rag—

knew I had only seconds until

pain returned, so took a photo—

the angle of my head, this neutral face.

UNCANNY VALLEY

I burst the arils from their pomegranate brain.
Pins of red on pyjamas.

The apron finally taken down from its hook,
my face covered in pinprick red—
Couldn't this be a vast opportunity?

Might be handy to look axe murderer abject
Might be handy to look

blithe in the face of crime; a robot
belief that nothing

should be quite like itself, not even murderously.
And this fruit almost a red brain

we should have bargained for in the garden;
unsliceable, lobed

and gnarled; ready for the story about how
what is false looks real.

PAINTING OF A FIELD BY VLAMINCK

Leaves have trafficked the unsaid and burst the blood-bag unexpectedly.

My friend years ago said there's a shade of red that gives her a headache.

Was it a red of nature or the reds of marketing or the red of known
        quantities?

We sat on either side of a nurse who drew our blood with impunity.

Near and far patches of orange where the field catches a person fainting in
        an elevator.

The specific obvious decaying to the lesser reminders ad infinitum, but then

You must deal with the flaming field while its red fades to noticeable orange.

Talking in the car about scary movies, enjoyable fear versus the unwatchable.

And the hill re-appears. The red arms of everything blot out air, ash, and
        lymph.

Or are the clouds—verdigris and aqua—a way of saying *I'm tired and*
        blacking out.

My friend reappears after her death. Standing in a yard, I have no idea how
        to say hi to her.

In the movie, a smoking battlefield morphs, a hundred years passing,
        into a meadow.

Waking up lying half out of an elevator: clouds sewn to the hill. Do we
        wake to death?

The fence that may be running through the grove steadies all: do we live
        to dream?

A crisp distance in autumn that may as well be full spring, the blood spring.

At night his arm around me, our veins full of unspoken things.

For years, the phrase   *when someone leaves an open field alone.*

FOR IF I AM NOT MISTAKEN, I HAVE BEEN (SI ENIM FALLOR, SUM)

The things that could be said about error

include estimated graves

wrong in number, not centered

in their proper plots.

Or miscounted bodies in mass graves.

Or miscounted dummies slung across a parapet, representing a battle.

Nearby gold-painted wheat offers

distraction, fronted

and forked with detritus.

Directors never sleep, they have to

wake up and oversee the fake blood,

what kind of wind will blow, which color smoke.

I can see by the way the trees beat

me at every game, beat you at every game,

beat us after so many dull days on the windowpanes

how quickly the truths are sweeping past.

On a circuit through close summer, back and forth

to the kitchen, the tea flakes constellating

in a glass, what I think is

experimental march music

is really

my roommate playing a video game.

You thought for the longest time

under the salved sorry stars

there was a bird misinformed about dawn.

We thought atoms were the smallest

as the scale of everything descended to zero

then regrouped to map vast pockets of *not sure what.*

I could hear scolding all day, daydreamed, and went to sleep,
dreamt I was at dinner:

A bustling mahogany table service:
too much everything. Blue wedges of ice.
Silver on the wrong side of a plate that
                              suddenly wasn't there.

Everyone, one by one, their voices
smashing into the walls, like a pilot who'd convinced himself

that not pulling up on the yoke was best
              they took turns
dismissing each of the other voices.

An error plants a space.

Entire trees burned to clear way for this movie.

A root-bound history hopeless in the ocean.

It's not really "I think therefore I am."

The saying isn't really, *To err is human.*

Actually, St. Augustine said, *For if I am not mistaken, I have been.*

I breathe, therefore I make mistakes

From mistake A to B, in the human scene:

I have no idea how all that dried blood got between my two toes.

I turned in the key to your house to my landlord by mistake—

Prove you are alive. *I have a social security card.*

Prove you are alive. *I have lost it.*

Wait: actually— actually, Augustine actually said *I have deceived,*

therefore I am.

Cotton poly with ink made of god knows what thrown in the river.

Tuft and lull, beggar and bigger.

I can think about what fits in this sack all day and not get better.

I claimed I could hear the dead in Siberia.

I could hear the conversation whispered in the back of my classroom

and shushed it.

Impossible reach, you win—

turning out ideas separated from truth.

An irrelevant order.

An impression something

held all this together in order   or does it—

In my life, I thought this one thing would happen, and this other thing

                 happened instead.

I can admit it was not twelve kinds of green in symphony.

I can admit the fractals hammered.

I can admit I was deceived

and therefore learn to make this new dish but with less and less

from what is known—

crumbs added, this closest substitute to reality.

CHINA KEEPS FINDING
MILLIONS OF PEOPLE WHO
NEVER OFFICIALLY EXISTED

Who feels like registering? I personally taped up the webcam

before you even tried to put a post-it on it.

Something about the girls being outnumbered

and illicit pottery leaving the country, nothing truly antique allowed

outside the boundaries. The laws about saying

they're here. *We're here.* I'm staring into space recollecting a country

where not a single man looked like my father but his sister

was him made over in worry and steam. Another story, herself.

I'm mastering a game of sticking with the subject

by only looking at objects in my peripheral vision.

Built this life on the remarks others made, their quasi-understandings

and from that and some pickled cabbage tried to make the old country.

The time my white roommate got angry because I seemed not to know

it's the one place where the men outnumber the women,

they had pushed so many baby girls down to die in the snow.

What I wouldn't give now to scoop up one of them. I constantly

woke that roommate up while ruining five spice stew

with rancid baking soda. Or alphabetizing, for no reason, the many books.

MARGINAL + PLEASANT

Red dotted sign above the bus driver flashes an optional intersection,
   the intersection of calm and off to the side.

At first, riding the bus, I thought this meant my kind or me. But then,
   Celeste said, *Almost everyone I know lives there.*

Turning from one wall to another with a mug of coffee in hand.

Someone posts: *My older son's cat looks like this and he's made a religion of him.*

Said to Celeste, *What's it like not to drink and not to have children*
   even though mid-life we both don't do or have either.

But eleven days of 45 and everyone's borderline exhausted, eating medicinally
   healthy food: pho chicken soup, curry, beans and rice and pork.

I watched the video about putting ice cream, M&M's and chocolate syrup
   in a bullet blender, then adding a lot of vodka and suddenly I
   understood the Russian people.

Years of 45 and we're floating in small spaces around doom, uncertain how
   to annihilate so much deliberate evil. How love could
   win against this.

The immeasurably thick wall between my past confidence in a rational
   nature and the current stupefaction at its rot.

A rational brother who taught me how to count out change, estimate

        the cost of groceries. Who taught me not to stand in the middle

        of the sidewalk while looking at one's cash.

The religion of not falling for the latest thinking, but relying on numbers

        and unexpected factors— lies such as *liberals have all the guns.*

I pick out the softest memory and try to text him a photo of it.

The stuffed bear I have that saved him in an earthquake and in a

        helicopter crash. Tell him, *my friend had to put a kitten down,*

        so lent her Felix.

I took a nap like that, rinsed my mind clear, set the amber lights anew,

        and I made a religion out of it, one I wasn't sure I could practice.

No matter what you say, the body wins, etc.

My brother who told me there's arsenic in apple seeds *but it won't hurt*

        you until you eat about half a cup.

COPIES

I spend a lot of time wishing they would invent the transporter beam so I could beam home, fry my mother a turmeric egg, spread cheese on her toast, beam back here, work. Beam 670 miles back to kiss her goodnight.

The scientist on the documentary says that if you want to beam to another place through quantum physics you will be *entirely* destroyed, the original version will always be destroyed.

I had looked into crowds in Beijing for ages and no one looked like Dad. They all did exercises and filed endlessly in a gesticulating line. Now he lives in my hands, my decisions at meetings, my bracing a plant to a chopstick with yarn.

He sits on a sofa in my dreams and, with his eyes, confirms ironies.

How many times have I set the copy machine to *scan*, not been sure the information has been sent because I cannot remember if an extra button has to be pressed.

Over and opal, the waxing of binary. To replace the blank paper and hit the green moon. Things to control; things controllable. And all that is so uncontrollable: wind, blind mind, forgetting, sinking, missing the moment.

Naturally, I cannot recreate my parents' whole journey across the ocean.

Seeing my parents grow old, I had wanted to have a baby with science and everyone seemed to think this was my depression talking, even the doctor.

I used to say I'd name her Cindy Junior because it seemed ridiculous *and* perfect. An ex yelled at me for an hour because he was a "Junior" and that practice, in fact, is narcissism.

Years later I dreamt of a doll in an old General Store. She said *take care of me*, and we all know what happens if I tell this from the point of view of the doll.

I see the Chinese American kids on YouTube eating fast food Chinese, complaining in vocal fry *how disgusting*. Their parents eat the exact same thing, say *it's good*, nothing more, and compliment the chef.

DEEPFAKE

What is the uncanny valley? asks the student and I draw the graph on the board, and point to the lowest point, and then move up the slope; *This is like a scarecrow, it's kinda shaped like a human but you're not sure; This is where you'd put a mannequin on the graph, this is where you'd put, say, a lifelike sex doll, and right here where this dip is...that's where you would just reach for your knife.*

People go back to observations said from the 60's and say *wow, they were prophets.* Why do people think it's a prophecy when it's that things are not changing? The story hasn't evolved.

Tonight I was standing in the yard while the dog ate grass and surveillance planes took off and landed in the airfield. The caravan at 1AM blaring stereos, honking horns and yelling WAKE UP because the cops who killed Breonna Taylor still have their jobs and have not been charged.

When my brother and his wife say through the open window of the truck that the video was fake— because the girlfriend is silent after they shoot her boyfriend, there's no way you could be silent then—I wonder how many faked videos they have seen at the same time that I wonder how they don't know she is silent out of terror.

My brothers taught me when I was little, while we watched cop shows, that a cop can shoot only in self defense. The other person has to shoot first, otherwise the cop can't touch them.

Today I read the headline that if you have an AI and enough photos of a person's face you can create news that seems real. That your likeness could be altered into what seems to be you. And this means that we have to rely on the people we know.

Where is the looking at the face? Where is the human wrinkle upon wrinkle that you cannot fake in any way. I feel that every time I see a face that makes my stomach hurt, I look below it and it says, "this is not a real person, this is a computer-generated person."

Your brothers tell you years in advance there's going to be a civil war. They say 2016 but it doesn't happen then. They say in April. But it doesn't happen then. It's just a lot of people believing an orchestration that alone would do nothing.

They say there's going to be trouble you should move up here or we'll bring you an automatic rifle. You say bring me an automatic baseball bat. Or a taser.

Do you know your neighbors? I ask one brother and he says he doesn't and he doesn't care about them, he only cares about his family, he just wants to protect them. And I think about how many people it takes to sew up a wound, and hours, and silence or low music, and so many hands to get the clamp and the daub and the stitches tight and effective.

My brother is worried that the other brother will get killed in a riot. Because do I know what the police started out as? Slave patrol, I say. But I don't understand how he's not worried that our brother will kill someone in a riot.

Who do you think I'm going to shoot when someone barges into the house?

Love thy neighbor versus know thy neighbor. Really know.

Rankine saying *I do projects instead of individual poems because I believe in historical moments.*

Because how could you possibly tell what is really happening in one moment? One needs a whole frieze, a whole constellation of moments to consider before the lies we are telling ourselves reveal themselves.

When I say to my brother through the open window of his truck *it seems like the cops are full of people from the KKK* and he and his wife laugh a weird high nervous laugh.

I remember getting struck by the rubber bullet and my entire body flooding with something more vivid than adrenaline, and putting my hand up, and looking at everyone to make sure I could walk off safely. My brothers looked out from behind their barrels and columns. I spent the rest of the afternoon watching them shoot my nephew, and each other.

Charity has the word for flesh in it.

Fussing at John back in the day because he never remembered to lock the door. Aren't you worried about intruders or robbers? And he grumbles, no, because to him danger *doesn't come from outside the house but inside the house.*

If you boil your father's life down to a thesis, what's the thesis? the interviewer asked me. I said, for mine, build something out of nothing. Kate said Learn by *doing.*

We don't practice for death, we practice for—

And years later, I think how you sometimes now can't tell if you're looking at the real thing or something false. The photo of the Capitol Hill Autonomous Zone barrier spliced with the photo of a masked man carrying an assault rifle. Or the Minneapolis precinct on fire being titled Seattle: Crazy City.

When I was 20, I told my dad I was going to the grocery store but I went to a friend's. I don't even remember why I told him that. I came home and went upstairs to where he was reading in bed. It was the first time I had really lied to him. He looked up from his book and said, "Where did you go?" and I said, "To the grocery." And he said, "Why are you lying to me?"

I don't tell my brothers what I think of their guns except that I tell them mom doesn't want them in her house. Instead I tell the one he's drunk the Kool-Aid and the other that he should be careful.

Elmer Fudd and Yosemite Sam will no longer use guns in their cartoons. What they will do instead? Hundreds of decals, t-shirts, cartoons, lunchboxes, underwear, sheets, in which they still carry a gun.

My brothers saying my dad thinking bb rifles were fine. That he was fine with guns. As if that's the same as the Kalashnikov you put in his closet. This isn't true.

I don't understand him anymore, Dad said to me so many times, *he thinks like a soldier.*

Mistrust of people who cannot understand a jasmine crown.
Mistrust of people who seem to be threatened.
Mistrust of people who send memes.

Stage acting is all about addressing the ghost of your father, and being in film is about silence.

How being a stage actor is a bouquet.
A film actor is the whole garden.

Dad saying *sometimes you can't tell if you are doing the right or wrong thing. Sometimes all you can do is pray.*

FACE BLINDNESS

They look at the photo and agree that's Dad in the class photo of Ip Man,
    wing chun master.

I look at the face and cannot say it looks like him to me.

My brother asked his forensics detective co-worker to look at the face.

Mom thinks it's him too, he says proudly.

My mother often watches gameshows and says *look it looks like*
    (insert neighbor)

and I look up to see some not even ballpark bone structure.

What was my father's face like when he left his country?

What was his face like when, alone, he made the pork and peas,
    washed socks.

This wretched neighborhood. When I say hi to white people on the street
    they don't say hi back. Chinese either.

Who has mastered this face, no sweeping lashes, just one naked thought
    after another.

The young people I think I smile at in a dark crowd who walk away as if
    my face said *you're standing in my way move along.*

I'd dress as Robert Smith or The Crow in high school and friends would say
    but you look normal that way.

I mention my Han melancholy, and you, my oldest niece, murmur *no,*
    grandpa told uncle DiDi we're Mongolian, I thought you knew?

You who had permission to deck any lump on the bus that called you tragic,
      or names.

I walk down the street feeling overly safe, I dgaf and want to magic you
      my extra.

But my face fails me with a weak best, what friends know as
      powered down mode.

What in the world is she thinking is what I sometimes ask myself,
      says a colleague about this face.

What a person sees of themselves, what partly disappears in the mirror.

FALLING DOWN

Who are these people that sleep with both eyes shut?
I asked you to tell me climbing would be foolish.

Further to fall.

In this suffocation, in this life you say
it's best to say *I'm fine* before hitting the earth.

You check my suitcase before I travel, pulling out a packet of needles,
safety pins, loose matches, saying *let's pull out the knives.* Lifelong,

I practice falling away from the sword

                      the edge a word   faking death   landing it

both eyes open, how bees sleep at night
despite my falling down stairs as a kid, bruises on legs— as an adult
ripping each
shoulder on black ice,

                          good at this—

Dawn blasting, the pink snow soon balances to white.
Smooth, the night underneath the daylit needles vibrates a black liquor.

Night will fall without rapture, us breathing despite everything,

marrow reverberating
faith riding a dot.

THE DISAPPEARING JACKET

Han Solo drops into the pit, his shirt white in one shot,
a black jacket in the next,

          then back to the white shirt.

Instead of "I love you too," he says, "I know."

A mistake that a whole bleary-eyed team had overlooked—
      an entire screening audience—
      an entire manufacturer of copies fails to pause—
      a whole machine looking in the wrong direction.

We watch a film to pass the time, for background noise as we iron.
Tell ourselves stories again and again, and chorus along
      to dialogue known by heart. Whatever it was, in childhood—
      steam in the carbonite pit—

the story and ourselves got middle-aged.

*

Once upon a time a spell meant to protect the tale had sent you to sleep.
Toward dreams.

Now, the spell feels hard to enter.
It blinds you to the fact of neighbors.
It seems uphill to ask *do you need this old windshield?*

Molly wrote, *In a story, the first to die are the ones who don't tell stories—*

Years ago, the neighbor told you when your father disappeared,
      Oh he got locked out, he's been sitting on our sofa.

*

Locked out.
That little denial before you relax and see how it can be solved.
So easy to adjust to the green lights in the doorways.

They fixed this gaffe in later versions cropping the mistake
faking a close-up of his face.

Orange light on black passing for orange light on white.
The white hat and black hat long obsolete.

*

The black collar-popped garment, painted on the action figure you used to
throw in the tub. From a small neon yellow fishing boat floating past
avocado flower decals. The full black element of a garment that says *we've
got this covered*, whatever your parents don't want to talk about: the year
they were born, the suicide of their brother, the actual time the shells
bombed the street and killed their dog. It's like, *tell you what, instead we'll
take you to a space opera*. No movie is ever complete until you find out how
alien cities and laser blasts were faked from a few upside down buckets, one
guy-wire in the Mojave that lost its dampeners. In my thirties, I longed for
a regular day, sitting in shade eating a snack and reviewing an old movie
I've seen dozens of times. And now, my brothers decide that I'd be better
off with an automatic rifle than a pistol. I can shoot a pistol right into the
smallest circle on the chest of a paper man. *But you won't have time*, they say.
You'll do better if you have to cover the front door.

*

When I was small, my brothers would send me out of the room when
Deerhunter, or *Platoon*, or *Full Metal Jacket* came on cable.

They don't realize that who threatens me is not who they think
threatens me.

Who wipes the rag across the dust, polishing the story when History can't
handle the needle of the actual. My brother telling me not to go to
California because the earthquake that's coming is too risky, and I go stare
at the cholla fields. Later thinking about thread, picking up the needle,
remembering how to sew.

As a kid, by day, I imagined characters as my friends;

By night, they played the other side of the game, dialogue
from the mutual mind.

Characters trained to make conversation from the slanted hall light,
who were company in the dark sheerly because I was supposed to be asleep.

Centuries are really cool, good for them.
They buff away the infernal dents so slowly it's as if
they make humans from scratch— from the scratches.

DEATHLESS

What are we going to do with you all?
No house, no job you wanted, but never dying.

You brought down napkins, diamonds, bars of soap,
Evangelical churches, and being buried. You ship

characters in an online multiverse. Cryogenics sold to you
and sensors, hormone therapy to add fifty years

to your life. Aged, gathered in an abandoned mall food court
eating what dropped out of a machine—

Mennonites drape dresses over a clothesline, what they wore on the beach.
It takes me a second to recall why my brother wanted to canoe

around a man-made lake. To feel the water push back.
Fish introduced, deer listening. A soil hurled at my feet

in excruciating slowness, the end. We rowed
into sunburn, knew to jab deep and try to pull through.

No one, when I asked them in their hospital sick beds, ever
wanted me to leave the TV on, no one wanted an artificial heart.

ALL THE TEARS

There is no secret sad thing to eviscerate.
I've pulled the glass lamps to me
and really no tears crawl there.

A clean interpretation of the fixtures:
nothing to distract but clarity and brightness.
Who cares about the reproduction beach,

the setting right there in a magazine breakfast nook:
What's the collection overall of preoccupations—
I'm so sure you'd still be here if I weren't

a column of light. I myself a consequence of light.
A shadow, of late. A boy dribbles for ten,
twenty, thirty minutes out front. Bam, bam, bam.

Where have we left the big nails?
I want to put a nail in the boy's basketball
while I take stock, all my tears:

Today Pam at her desk laughing harder—
harder than I ever heard her.
Or the scintillating blue-green of sedan,

the hang of clouds
versus the poise of houses,
those beautifully thrown dice

so out of reach. How
to stab the moment
during the wind-dreams
of these trees. How fast—

laugh this all to sleep by never falling asleep.
He said, *Okay is the new fabulous.*
How fast until the next beautiful random

that mends the pattern to *things*
as they are? That sound like a rocket taking off,
the class all staring at the ceiling.

MORNING, AS IS

I didn't want to do it over in silk flowers
the main strands of staying here—
flowers made of yarn held behind the back,
a shore where splendor washed up
a glittery stone, a sun setting in its stripes.
I threw it back, threw back the stone
sleeping its two dreams in my hand
but also awake   it splashed as I threw it back
and my friend cried out
as if this left things less complete.

BEFORE THE PARTY

To dream of being elsewhere and here at the same time.
To imagine the party and later, hear a knock that interrupts
        and go answer the door.

To know that the party is difficult, at first, for everyone.
How often one is not asked what one is, where one is from.
I study waterlines in the river,
count off the boats as each passes with strangers.

Melody out of its context,
some unanswerable figment or fragment that hangs
over the soon-on lights.

The way afternoon lays them all out together,
a vased forsythia ready for more water.

Out the window, they were throwing plantable hair,
bundled grass-like hair.

Grass sparkled, grass blue down to the East River,
Hasidim in Burberry high-necked blouses
chased their kids and their kids' yarmulkes and curls.

I was trying to solve the problem of where to begin—
here, where each cable of the bridge needs replacing,
where the necessary trains run rarely, or never, these
arms the gesture of futility where the woman
and man walk the street in a bridal gown and tux.

Getting married, taffeta strong, concrete as hard.
The sign covered with white. No one can believe
a supposition that time could bend back to itself.
I hear friends announce a wedding, and hurrying
at the window to let in everything, doors open for normal life.

From here, I can see the Manhattan Bridge.

White wire frantic in tension, the arcs laddered.

Remember Brett, drunk, climbed the pilings, called

seven states at two a.m. from the cold metal

between his legs, wind lashing his hair?

A total vertigo and that's enough. Grand piano

overlooking the East River, some gunwales,

Whitman's firehouse. Jared plays the piano.

The gasoline-fire-sunset extinguished hours ago, hours—

so long ago it's mid-day. It's a long tinkling ladder.

Music already known in the pianist's mind. Nothing a surprise.

Maybe a chord throws you into the sky. The next tethers you back again.

My friend's insistence on never being on time to parties,
but playing one last stormy song on the piano.

I sit on the couch listening to Jared play a tune
and imagine the composer thirty years before capturing
a kind of spontaneous aesthetic curl.

The maker made, the new man playing.

Zero sense that a pianist loves the climb of notes: they appear in the air.

They're late for the party. People as notes.
I am staying here to nap while my friends walk out.

Long walk to the closet.
Long walk to an arrangement of clean water glasses.
Long walk to wash hands.
I touch cotton, my friend has brought a coral sheet to throw over this
afternoon.

Staring out the window at the bridge, all broad actual traffic noted.

Farrah shuffles to the bedroom. Gives thought to her preparations.

The recalled cartoon is hilarious: a man on a cell phone says,

"I am on the train, I am getting off the train, I am off the train."

I am on the platform, I am getting on the train, I am on the train
and befriending the old skinny couple taking
the same rerouting I had to take.

How about this air-conditioning? the old man asked. *I remember*
when the train would run from 6th street with the doors

                                     open and one fan blowing at the end.

This mind leaps to whatever year it wants. How will it be
when the trains are gone?

He and his wife look like senior citizens robbed of their clothes
and given clothes to match an inner youth.

Keeping up with each mirror.

I recall waking at dawn and reading 102 comments on an article
about regret:

The man who left his father's deathbed to finish a report at
Morgan Stanley;
how he wishes he had just walked out of the office that day.

The woman who stayed with her terrible boyfriend
who then left her childless forever.

Something like reading through essays about mothers who
slap and handle their grown daughters.

My student who writes about a friend making her promise
never to tell and showing her
a garbage bag that stinks and saying *I had a baby*
and I look up from the essay
and don't know who to tell or whether to at all.

I think of thinking-on-the-subway.

Farrah throws the butt of a scarf over her shoulder before me.

I decide to make schemata on being in two places at once:

Liminal space of telephone talk,

walking sand at the water's edge, standing in the doorway.

Lintel and handset.

Is where the land and the sea meet really literature?

Is half of one thing and half its opposite tossed together really a story?

      I think of Chopin, I think of Satie.

      My friend's hands press out notes.

      Home mists to omission.

      They're leaving for the party. I imagine it—

      the almost-pain of saying goodbye quickly,

      the other person's eyes already elsewhere.

I had not counted on the sound of
reeds ticking together, the white gulls
planted in the green. Right now, in the city.

They say browns and blacks against mostly white
           trick you into thinking
you are looking at a dream/in a dream.

Thinking of the great paintings of snow: what symbol
underneath?
What symbol of white over symbols of everything?

Liminal gestures: seeing pattern and choosing
gray as a backdrop;
every color looks good against gray,
every musical note a gray bone.

A gray nation floundering down until it gets a spray
of bright orange at its throat.

When you first arrive and stand
by the forty-spice party hummus, you dream
of an alleyway where no one can notice you.

This wisdom of taking forever to get out the door.
        Opening and shutting of drawers.

A word is a drawer:

Scarf. Subway. Recollection. Leaving. Melody.

A limit, a border places you on the river edge, sheet music on a park bound-
ary.

        I don't know what happened in that dream except
        my brother gave me advice while he was
        a panda drowning in light. Or a bison. An almost Buddha.

        The field stood still and rippled its reeds.

We're always looking for the maker's sleeve

while the thing itself is the mind

the thing itself is a blueprint

in which to measure or be lost. They say:

No maker but in the made.

I ask Jared with his fingers tinkling out on keys

who wrote that – this friend who knows every writer, every painter.

Out in Manhattan, the clouds shade something unseen from here.

He says *I was making it up as I went along.*

MONUMENTS OF LIGHT
THE OPEN SIGNS

The shops each had an open sign in red and blue
One hung, a dotted oval of red around blue letters
Another spun dotted blue letters within a red oval

I feel the desperate angles of a gunman shooting into my dream
Red blue red blue sirens full cups of silver
I pull my mother's arm and yell for her to duck:

Monuments of light to insight. Moments of lightness
opening the doors of ears, to the navel, to the toes
opening the doors to the Laundromats, to the drugstores

to the trees roping all Florida day, open a teacup
the orange in manage; an unlocked door flips open
the sign on, deep in the pine night, so much

a futurist campsite. The cars of dreams wreck
the passports in dreams always misplaced
the airplanes have taken off and family

drive suitcases slow-mo to a plane that's never caught.
Walking back to my real office, I hear a woman mumble
slowly to her open phone: *I had terrible dreams last night.*

Slowly to the air these messages open, an alarm
like fire. *Open the light* as they say in French. *Face the light—*
say the store exits and that door—wide open, is open

INVISIBILIFY

This drowned thought
the cab has asthma becomes
the car has arms— and later
the flowers dried out
the lilies go bomping
(the phone wanted to simplify)
Mom can't recall that I was here
I look up tricks for keeping
forgetful people calm:
put objects where they belong
wash the years off their faces
buy them peridot
show them the letter
in which their father begs
the mother to buy
some bread or
show them a star that rides in its blue case
a small fire that sets every evening
and appears in this green order
moons of this life
flung into sunshine

CARRIED OUT

Two things happened today, now lost in the white headache. Wind shakes impermanent flags. Today I texted a baby that I was cranky, I must need a nap. Today I downloaded the sound of rain and whales, those large dreams drifting through the saline. Delved into an idea about being in the same room. As what. As darkness or a swift contentedness. The known but unseen, unmanifested. I said this thing, it wasn't the action of eating an apple, or seeing— maybe it wasn't mere talking. Flowers caressing up the sky might have been it. The baby noises, that's my friend's baby learning the pace, how to connect her naps. My mother considered my reading about childrearing redundant. She says, *Weren't you there in the first place? Sing "Edelweiss" at the sight of tears, say "the sun is shining" for sad lip.* These clotted brights are goners. The starved polar bear, this closet. To move through one more darkened room or field to help something helpless.

I followed my mother, once, through a museum where everything surpassed her. This morning, I stood at my father's grave and wept. I had pointed out the way to its blunt face, my mother driving the cemetery roads only knowing to turn when I said to. History does better in her old house, her post-its on the leashes, the old face cream, but outside its walls, she can't remember the story. She says to me, *I need you to help me, I need a mama.* I think of but don't say a joke that goes: *Good thing we'll be here at your funeral, good thing you'll have a driver, that no one will lose you, or ask you to find your way to this spot.*

POEM

Ocean. One perceivable star.
Blue burnished, close.
A pink collar hangs around
new horizon. I turn my head
and scope the sunset. I turn
my head and note darkness
doing its nightly boast.
Scan the sky, find the star—
first star. So pinpoint,
so answer. Look to its side,
see it. But then any blue
patch offers the thing: a point,
a pin, a white conflagration
far enough to mean little
and soon all the stars
are out. They burn
and I recall the poem
in which I cannot find
you. No one motion
can break the camera
so high over the beach.
The baseball chucked
directly up twists in
for a close-up. The
orderlies far off
in winter, are clean
indifferent to a number
I cannot recall but
looking in this high-rise
for your room, I need
it. And everyone flips
through strangers' X-
rays. The exact population
of stars means little
to them. The exact
address where I

need to be no one
knows. They keep
saying your place
isn't a room, but
a kind of paragraph.

ABSENCE

The sun streamed strongly into the room from somewhere but I was
haunting it from the attic hatch in the ceiling. I kept seeing myself down
underneath in the bedroom. Moving gold rimmed tea sets. Folding laundry.
No matter what I did, I couldn't quite make eye contact with the me living
below. I tried to get my own attention. I put on a green corduroy dress in
my favorite color, rotting boots like dirt, I traded my hair in for fire, I took
my face out so there was nothing there. Below, other me was witless,
looking to the left and right; Attic me was scaring the crap out of real life
living room me. But real life me could never actually catch a glimpse of
ghost me, no matter how hard I whipped around, I only ever caught the
edge of flames or the window of nothing where the face had been. What
had I done with my life to make my future dead self so profesh at menace?
Guests sipped tea, nodded, pretended to believe that I was being haunted. I
wanted to reach down from the attic and steal something from me as proof.
The way you might steal a cardigan from a sibling thinking it's wasted
on her, it would look better on me—as if it's wasted on me, I mean—this
world/this I that I/that the rest of us kept using so poorly.

SOFTNESS

One week   Out of nothing & nowhere

Up rose the word *soft* for everything

Paige let's not sit in the back room, the front one is softer

like pears, but the avoidance of peril

Air soft

Ice   blood soft

This word tying a bow

When I sit in front of everyone, it feels softer than being between them

It's my mysterious   not a cut   not a wound

Getting worse   no spider in sight

A always saying *in the next lifetime*

And I always say   *I'm not coming back here*

The soft placement of the useful   to a useful silhouette

I'll be fine as the wind or a piece of grass

R says *I would like to be a pine cone*

Resting on grass   easy start of a forest

H was asking me how it felt to ring the gong

Hold space   be silent

In this particular way   I said a few words and he wondered

Is there another one   I said *softness*

He said *that is the literal meaning for metta or kindness*

How far to send a hammer behind the eyes

When you can send   a softness

Let slip what isn't an actor

Never one to press the head too hard to the fever—

DOOR TO A FOREST

How jalapeños feel in your mouth after they've softened in the pan. That green peppers softened the same way/in your mouth are almost but not the same. You try to invent a new recipe but the flavor of bamboo, green pepper, pork, dofu gan, that your old Chinese blah blah blah made, scent creeping upstairs as you hashed out math symbols: this all forms nostalgia in front of your face. You start the thought again. Soft green plus a different soft green. You start again. Something clear as vodka or bells. Egg cooked with sesame, chili oil, seeds all settled with salt. This may not be available as you become more elderly. You try to cut nostalgia at the roots. All these years, you've been sequencing and gathering. These green thoughts steep into a real forest. You step behind the house you live in inside your mind. Over the course of nights, people meet you there as if they are simply living on the other side of a curtain. People so real you picture them while walking down the hall IRL. But it hangs there unseen each night when you dream, or whatever is happening that allows you to meet the leaves cool on your face, something not alive and not dead that you've walked through for ages.

DE BEAUX RESTES

It means to have
beautiful leftovers.
Not food but the body's
look in old age.
Mom always says
Robert Redford looks
like *une vieille pomme*
an old apple
though he has
de beaux restes.
I'm aware how often
I say my *mom used to*
or *my dad used to,*
that there's no one
to pass my hair down
to. That this apple
stain which might have been
the blood of a dinosaur clears away
with enough hot water.
The futon by itself in Philly.
I'm watching a spy
movie from the 70's
in my hometown
on a Sunday, a channel
I can't get anywhere
else. Pretty sure
I'm going to go out
of this life scrambling after
facts: the times I did so
and you managed
in the code of people
who understand everything
to look away. Robert
Redford comes
back from getting
his lunch and all
his coworkers

lie shot. I think
so often of when the
roads stayed out of view,
when I curled in
the backseat
of the car, too small to look
out the window.
I totally get how you
want to lean things
together in a field
of nothing. The two
sides of things seem
utter vapor. You
probably also were
a kid so quiet, they
came to the door
to say, *you still alive?*
Sometimes my mom says,
I wish dad were here so I
could fight with
him. Robert Redford
dials an untraceable
phone and when
he finds out it's all
an inside job, my
mom says, *This*
is a terrible movie.
Maybe it's
nostalgia that
creates the essential
nothing. For the people
we thought could
hold the cellphone
while we found
a shrub to use
in the park, now
departed. Now

Robert Redford
asks his boss
who had been
trying to kill him
in the big tell-off
moment, quote,
Are we really
planning to invade
The Middle East
for oil? When the film
came out, everyone
thought the movie
was crap and had
no substance. For
fuck's sake now I'm
suspicious of even
the apples. No roads
go pewter calm.
I've seen you tell
a roomful of parents: *this*
is what happened
when I asked your
children to make
a pencil speak.
When friends
are not around
which is often,
I watch celebrities
reveal their souls
on YouTube.
Robert Redford
his face not quite
gone to hardwood.
You're gonna die
a very lonely man,
they tell spy Redford
when he throws their

interior conspiracy
and all its lurking
detail to the *Times*.
You're right, an utterance
is still worth it
even if it hangs
out in the open,
a coral pendant.
A verb to be we're
inclined to show.
I remember the
literal flies tapping
on the window.
Robert Redford
does look like
an old apple
though the *beaux*
restes means well-
preserved, not leftovers.
You've probably seen
a doll with a dried
apple for a head
and pretended it
could hear. Who the hell
is there to tell but
quiet people? The terrible
leftovers I didn't
throw out that you
must have seen. I felt
confirmed in my
trying to have a baby when
I realized what huge
bags of food I kept giving
you. Redford's hidden
sorrow he wouldn't
even tell his biographer
about, the writer who

followed him
for 14 years (that his first baby
died a crib death).
I think that's what's
inside good acting:
the not pretending. I think,
in the movie, that
line about *you're gonna die*
a lonely man—
that simple lie— those
are the open windows
of being alive.

NOTES

The poem "Continuity" draws from scenes in the documentary *A.K.* by Chris Marker which I first saw on KQED in the 90s. The documentary features behind the scenes footage of the making of *Ran*, and my poem in particular draws from images that feature Teruyo Nogami, Akira Kirosawa's continuity assistant.

"Veil from Anapos" is after an eponymous painting by Sam Messenger.
"Jiu Jitsu Déçu" is dedicated to Rachel Bunting. It refers to the death of
   Melissa Ketanuti.
"De Beaux Restes" is for Stephanie Cawley.
"Hope is the Mother of the Stupid" is a Polish proverb used by
   Kyle Coma-Thompson on IG.

ACKNOWLEDGMENTS

I would like to thank the editors and guest editors of the following journals for publishing these poems, sometimes in other versions:

"Before the Party" "Hope is the Mother of the Stupid" and
"invisibilify" *diode*
"All My Creys" *Drunken Boat*
"Veil from Anapos" *Nöo Journal*
"Painting of a Field by Vlaminck" *Fanzine*
"Continuity" and "Copies" *The Georgia Review*
"Door to a Forest" "Absence" and "China Finds Millions of People Who
       Never Existed" *jubilat*
"For if I am Not Mistaken, I Have Been," *Long Poem Journal*
"Jiu Jitsu Déçu" *OnandOnscreen*
"Everybody Thinks They are the Good Guy" and "Face Blindness" *Poetry*
"De Beaux Gestes" *Powderkeg*
"Stillness" "Carried Out" and "[so from screaming it turned into things
      like blaming it all] *Sink Review*
"Poem [Ocean. One Perceivable Star.]" *PEN American Blog*

Special thanks for editorial help and inspiration goes to Jesseca Cornelson, Thomas Devaney, Emari DiGiorgio, Kyle Coma-Thompson, Soham Patel, and Evan Chen. Thanks to Zachary Schomburg and Mathias Svalina for all their support over the years, and thanks to Harper Quinn for being such a phenomenal editor and profoundest of listeners. Everyone deserves such poetry therapy. Thanks to Ken Miranda and Laura Jaramillo for the final touches and support.

Much appreciation to the students and teachers of Squaw Valley Community of Writers in Squaw Valley, California and to the cabin crew Rachel Bunting, Donna Voyerer, Mike Nees, and Donna Huneke.